IF ALL
VACATION

Written by Brianna Ellis
Illustrated by Arabella Rb

Copyright © 2025 Brianna Ellis

All rights reserved.
No portion of this book may be reproduced or used in any form without the prior written permission of the copyright owner, except for the use of brief quotations in a book review.

For more information, contact:
Email: Briannae913@gmail.com

ISBN: 979-8-9913540-7-3

First edition printed in 2025.

Illustrated by Arabella Rb

Dedication

**To those who struggle
with the weight of negative emotions.
All jokes aside, your mental health matters.
You deserve healing and inner peace.**

**After a peaceful meditation,
I had this striking revelation.
What if all my problems packed up
and went on their own vacation?**

For a while, I contemplated how to approach the conversation. Anxiety is quite the drama queen, and Fear ignites frustration.

Let's not get started on Anger.
He has a very short fuse!
Unworthiness is overwhelming,
so I have nothing left to lose.

I'm tired of each and every issue,
but Anger makes me feel the sickest.
I finally gathered up the strength
to book them one-way tickets.

The next day, I sat my problems down—an awkward convo in my kitchen. As I expressed the shocking news, Unworthiness was guilt-stricken.

Anxiety said she was unsure,
and needs more time to overthink it.
Fear and Anger exploded into rage,
then started power tripping.

Just by witnessing their reactions, I knew this was the best decision. Tomorrow, they're off to Unbearable Island. Trust me, I promise I won't miss them!

I told Fear not to send a postcard.
Anger, don't bother to text or call.
Anxiety made me feel a little guilty,
so I took them all to the mall.

I even bought them tropical outfits for their final destination.
My problems think they're coming back next week,
but are in for a rude awakening.

The next morning, I woke up early to give each one a warm goodbye. Unworthiness felt undeserving. Anxiety was quick to cry.

Anger said I was to blame,
while Fear tried to instill shame.
Sadly, we were inseparable for years,
but now it's time to make a change.

With pure love, I released pain and bade my problems a farewell. I hope they have a pleasant stay at the Healing Heart Hotel.

Why do we form toxic attachments to our negative emotions?
Instead of sitting in this feeling, I cleansed my body in the ocean.

For the first time in forever,
I didn't need wine to unwind.
Just some tea to feel at ease-
safe and secure in my own mind.

My problems are of the past.
They're having a blast on the island.
Unworthiness sent me a picture
of Fear and Anger actually smiling!

I feel alive and energized-grounded in my inner peace. Goodbye Anger, farewell Fear, Unworthiness and Anxiety.

Thankfully, Unbearable Island
is their permanent location.
For peace of mind and relaxation,
book your problems a vacation.

Made in the USA
Coppell, TX
14 February 2026